For Chris, Olivia, and Will—
always your ultimate fan xx.
—W.L.

For Lucia and Marcel, you are
the best thing that's ever been mine.
—E.C.

Text copyright © 2023, 2024 by Wendy Loggia
Cover art and interior illustrations copyright © 2023, 2024 by Elisa Chavarri
All rights reserved. Published in the United States by Golden Books, an imprint of
Random House Children's Books, a division of Penguin Random House LLC,
1745 Broadway, New York, NY 10019. Originally published in a slightly different form
as *Taylor Swift: A Little Golden Book Biography* by Golden Books, an imprint of
Random House Children's Books, a division of Penguin Random House LLC, New York,
in 2023. Golden Books, A Golden Book, A Little Golden Book, the G colophon, and the
distinctive gold spine are registered trademarks of Penguin Random House LLC.
rhcbooks.com
Library of Congress Cataloging-in-Publication Data is available upon request.
ISBN 979-8-217-03128-3 (trade)
Printed in the United States of America
10 9 8 7 6 5 4 3 2 1

a Little Golden Book® BIOGRAPHY

TAYLOR SWIFT
ULTIMATE FAN EDITION

By Wendy Loggia
Illustrated by Elisa Chavarri

A GOLDEN BOOK • NEW YORK

Taylor Alison Swift was born on December 13, 1989, in West Reading, Pennsylvania. Her parents named her after James Taylor, a famous musician.

A lot of love surrounded Taylor and her little brother, Austin. The Swifts did many activities as a family. They spent time reading books, visiting new places, and having fun outside.

Christmas was one of Taylor's holidays. And what made the holiday season even more exciting was that her family lived on a Christmas tree farm!

"I really love Christmas. I wish it was all year round."

Everyone pitched in at Christmastime. Taylor's dad mowed the fields on his tractor. Taylor's job? Picking praying mantis egg pods off the trees. The Swifts didn't want anyone to get a buggy surprise on Christmas morning!

As a kid, Taylor tried lots of different things. She rode horses. She acted in plays. She wrote poetry. But when she learned how to play the guitar, she knew she had found her passion.

When Taylor has a goal, nothing stops her! She was a big fan of country superstars Faith Hill and Shania Twain, and she discovered that both musicians had started their careers in Nashville, Tennessee.

That was all ten-year-old Taylor needed to know. She asked her parents to take her to Nashville. She asked them every day. And finally, when she was eleven, it happened! Her mom took Taylor and Austin there for spring break. They drove up and down Music Row—an area with country music recording studios and businesses. While Taylor's mom and brother waited in the car, Taylor ran into the offices of various record labels and handed out CDs she'd made of her music.

Taylor performed anywhere that would have her, including fairs, festivals, and ball games. But sometimes following dreams means doing things other people don't understand. Girls at school were mean to Taylor. Her classmates thought it was weird to like country music so much.

This made Taylor sad. But it didn't stop her from doing what she loved.

When Taylor was thirteen, something incredible happened. RCA Records wanted to work with her! Taylor and her family said goodbye to Pennsylvania and moved to Nashville. Her dream of being a country-music star was about to come true!

For Taylor, writing songs was just as important as singing them. But because she was young, the record company wanted her to sing other people's songs. And they thought she should wait until she was older before she made her own album.

Taylor didn't agree. One night, Taylor performed at Nashville's Bluebird Café. She sang some of her own songs and some songs from other singers. She caught the eye of a music executive in the crowd who was forming a new record label. Guess who he signed up to make an album? Taylor Swift!

Taylor's debut album, *Taylor Swift*, came out when she was just sixteen. She was excited every time she heard her songs on the radio! Her next album, *Fearless*, was the top-selling record of the year—and made Taylor a huge star.

Taylor *is* fearless. When she went on her first concert tour, she took the music world by storm!

One of Taylor's biggest strengths is storytelling—her songs tell stories that many people can relate to.

Taylor wrote all the songs on her third album, *Speak Now*. Listening to a Taylor Swift album is like hearing her diary being sung out loud!

Many of Taylor's songs are inspired by her life, like "The Best Day," a song about growing up in a loving family and having a supportive mom.

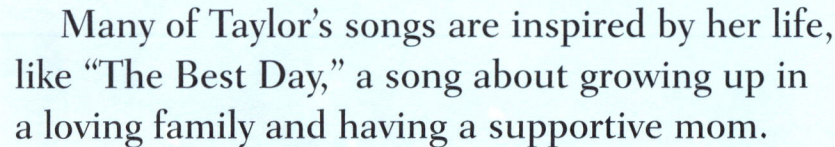

Taylor and her mom, Andrea, are very close. They talk about everything. No one has known Taylor longer—or knows her better—than her mom!

Trying new things and taking risks is important to Taylor. Even though country music was her first love, she took a big chance and recorded a pop album called *1989*—and it was the best-selling album of the year! Taylor never lets anything hold her back from creating music she loves.

Taylor also loves sharing things with her fans. They know that her lucky number is thirteen. She often hides clues and symbols in her music and videos. For a few of her albums, she surprised special groups of fans by inviting them to secret parties to listen to the album before anyone else. They got to hang out at her house, meet her family—and even bake cookies together!

When Taylor likes something, she tells everyone about it. One thing she really likes? Cats!

Taylor has a big reputation for speaking out against injustice and for encouraging people to vote. She stands up for other artists and herself, even when it's tough. She's not just a superstar—she's a trailblazer!

Taylor's hard work has paid off. Her albums have sold millions of copies. She has won multiple Grammys. She's traveled around the world and made people happy with her music. What will she do next?

When you're Taylor Swift, the sky's the limit!

TAYLOR SWIFT: SUPERSTAR!

Taylor has thrilled fans in all corners of the globe with her Eras Tour. Each night, she sings more than forty-four songs, plays guitar and piano, dances, and changes into about sixteen different outfits. The concert is more than three hours long and is divided into ten acts. Each act represents a different era of Taylor.

Turn the page to see which era you're in. . . .

THE ERAS QUIZ

Circle your answer to each question.

1. What is your dream dress-up outfit?
- A. anything pink
- B. a sparkly fringe dress
- C. a black bodysuit
- D. a flowy dress and cardigan
- E. a flared mini skater skirt and a cami top

2. Which song could you listen to all day?
- A. "Cruel Summer"
- B. "You Belong With Me"
- C. "Look What You Made Me Do"
- D. "invisible string"
- E. "Wildest Dreams"

3. Which word best describes you?
- A. dreamy
- B. country
- C. edgy
- D. vintage
- E. colorful

4. Which is your favorite emoji?
- A. butterfly 🦋
- B. sunflower 🌻
- C. snake 🐍
- D. leaves 🍂
- E. blue heart 💙

5. Which friendship bracelet would you trade for?
- A. IN MY FEELINGS with pale green, blue, lavender, and pink beads
- B. BRAVE with gold and white beads
- C. ICONIC with black and red beads
- D. AUGUST with gray, cream, and green beads
- E. STYLE with teal, navy, and silver beads

6. If you could see Taylor perform in one of these cities, which would you choose?
- A. London
- B. Nashville
- C. Chicago
- D. Boston
- E. New York City

THE ERAS QUIZ: RESULTS

If you picked mostly *As* . . . you're in your

Lover Era

If you picked mostly *Bs* . . . you're in your

FEARLESS ERA

If you picked mostly Cs . . . you're in your

reputation era

If you picked mostly Ds . . . you're in your

folklore era

If you picked mostly Es . . . you're in your

1989 ERA

MAJOR MASH-UPS

Taylor loves to surprise her fans with unexpected mash-ups during her concerts. Blending different songs together makes each performance unique. Here are some memorable surprise mash-ups from the Eras Tour:

"Is It Over Now?" and "Out of the Woods"

"White Horse" and "coney island"

"New Year's Day" and "Peace"

"Forever & Always" and "Maroon"

"Would've, Could've, Should've" and "ivy"

"Mine" and "Starlight"

"long story short" and "The Story of Us"

"Clean" and "evermore"

"Foolish One" and "Tell Me Why"

"This Love" and "Call It What You Want"

"Sparks Fly" and "gold rush"

"Begin Again" and "Paris"

"I Think He Knows" and "Gorgeous"

"Getaway Car," "august," and "The Other Side of the Door"

Which songs would you choose for a mash-up?

_____

and _____

♡ WORLD TRAVELER ♡

The Eras Tour has taken Taylor to cities all around the world. Were you lucky enough to go to her concert? Draw a heart next to the place or places you saw Taylor perform. Draw a star next to the places you've been to or would like to visit.

- [ ] Glendale, Arizona
- [ ] Las Vegas, Nevada
- [ ] Arlington, Texas
- [ ] Tampa, Florida
- [ ] Houston, Texas
- [ ] Atlanta, Georgia
- [ ] Nashville, Tennessee
- [ ] Philadelphia, Pennsylvania
- [ ] Foxborough, Massachusetts
- [ ] East Rutherford, New Jersey
- [ ] Chicago, Illinois
- [ ] Detroit, Michigan
- [ ] Pittsburgh, Pennsylvania
- [ ] Minneapolis, Minnesota
- [ ] Cincinnati, Ohio
- [ ] Kansas City, Missouri
- [ ] Denver, Colorado
- [ ] Seattle, Washington
- [ ] Santa Clara, California
- [ ] Los Angeles, California

- ☐ Miami, Florida
- ☐ New Orleans, Louisiana
- ☐ Indianapolis, Indiana
- ☐ Mexico City, Mexico
- ☐ Buenos Aires, Argentina
- ☐ Rio de Janeiro, Brazil
- ☐ São Paulo, Brazil
- ☐ Tokyo, Japan
- ☐ Melbourne, Australia
- ☐ Sydney, Australia
- ☐ Singapore, Singapore
- ☐ Paris, France
- ☐ Stockholm, Sweden
- ☐ Lisbon, Portugal
- ☐ Madrid, Spain
- ☐ Lyon, France

- ☐ Edinburgh, United Kingdom
- ☐ Liverpool, United Kingdom
- ☐ Cardiff, United Kingdom
- ☐ London, United Kingdom
- ☐ Dublin, Ireland
- ☐ Amsterdam, Netherlands
- ☐ Zurich, Switzerland
- ☐ Milan, Italy
- ☐ Gelsenkirchen, Germany
- ☐ Hamburg, Germany
- ☐ Munich, Germany
- ☐ Warsaw, Poland
- ☐ Vienna, Austria
- ☐ Toronto, Canada
- ☐ Vancouver, Canada

MAKING MEMORIES

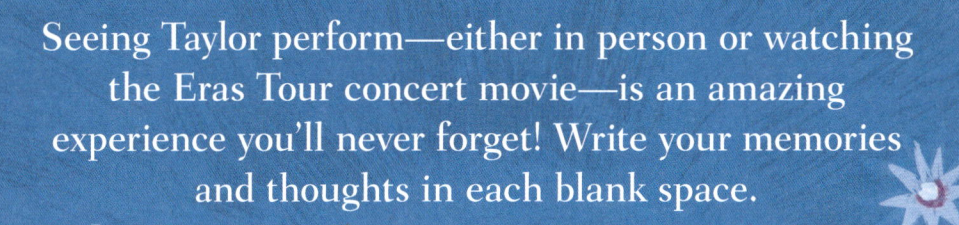

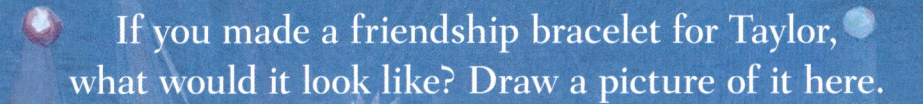

Seeing Taylor perform—either in person or watching the Eras Tour concert movie—is an amazing experience you'll never forget! Write your memories and thoughts in each blank space.

♥

If you made a friendship bracelet for Taylor, what would it look like? Draw a picture of it here.

What would you do if you got the "22" hat?
What would you say to Taylor?

Which part of the concert did you like best?

What do you love most about Taylor Swift?

What are your favorite songs?

1.
2.
3.
4.
5.
6.
7.
8.
9.
10.

Do you have confetti from the concert?
A ticket stub? A photo? Tape your collectibles here!

IT STARTED WITH A FRIENDSHIP BRACELET

If Taylor's in a stadium, you'd expect to see her on a stage singing, right? Not always! Since she started dating NFL player Travis Kelce, Taylor is often in the stadium seats cheering for the Kansas City Chiefs with the rest of the fans.

In July 2023, Travis went to the Eras Tour at Arrowhead Stadium in Kansas City, Missouri, hoping to meet Taylor and give her a friendship bracelet.

The two celebrities didn't end up meeting that night, but just two months later, they were officially a couple, and Taylor was sitting with Travis's mother at football games!

Taylor was there to celebrate with him when the Chiefs won the Super Bowl. And Travis went to a lot of her concerts!

YOU'RE A POET

Taylor has been writing poetry since she was a young girl. Poems—and song lyrics—can be about anything. They can be inspired by a true story or come from your imagination. They can be serious or funny.

Write a poem about someone special to you.

_____

_____

_____

_____

_____

_____

Write a poem about your dreams for the future.

TAYLOR SWIFT NEVER GOES OUT OF STYLE!

Use crayons or colored pencils
to decorate the outfits.

Add your favorite colors to these pictures.

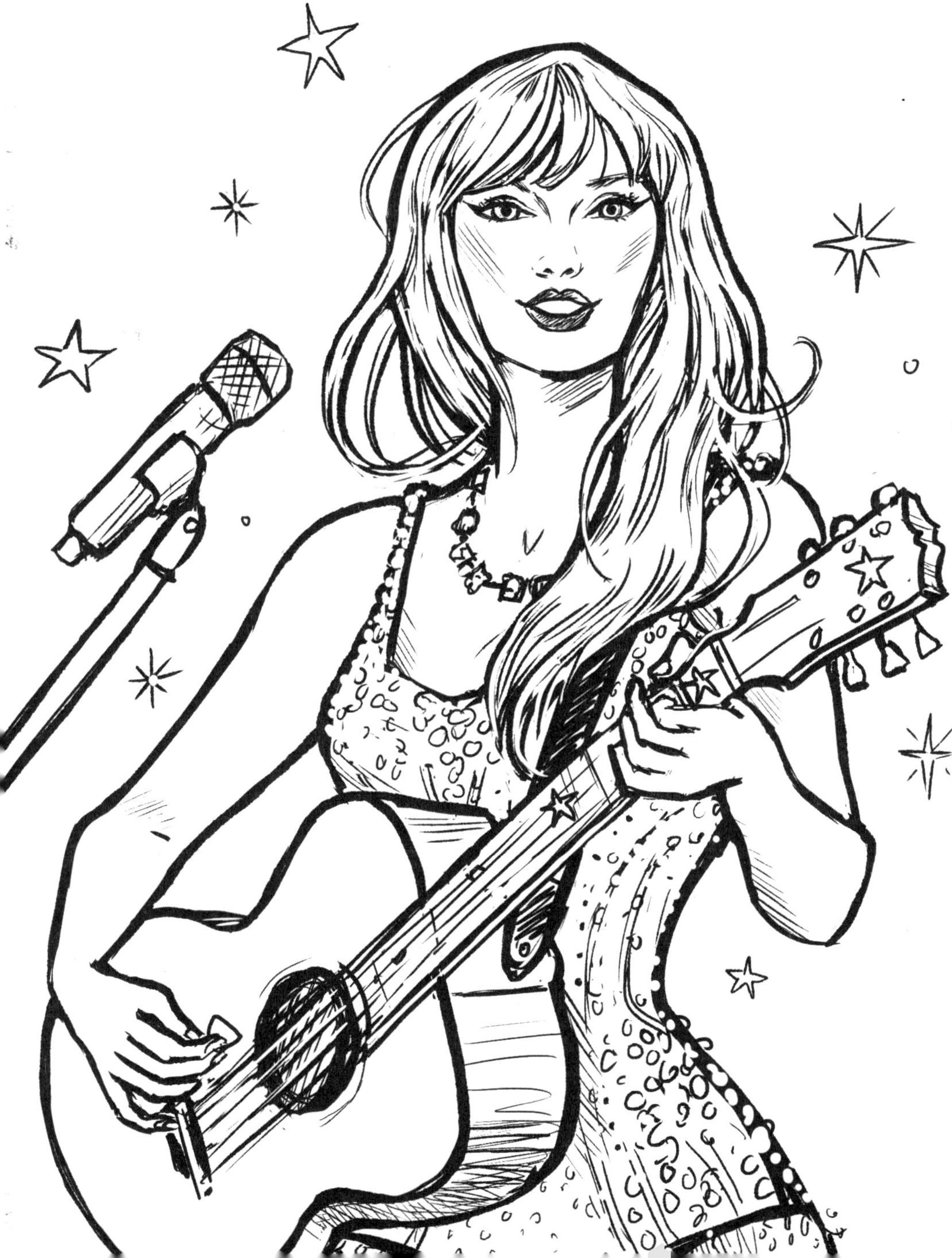

TAYLOR SAID IT!

"My job is to be an **ENTERTAINER.**"

"I feel a great amount of **GRATITUDE** that I was able to make music from the time I was a teenager."

"NEVER BE ASHAMED OF TRYING."

"You should celebrate who you are now, where you're going, and **WHERE YOU'VE BEEN.**"

"Hard work pays off. **ALWAYS.**"

© Elisa Chavarri

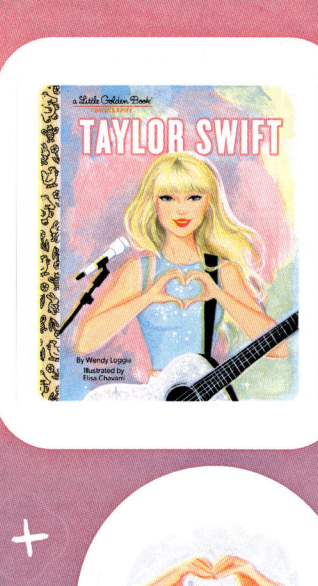